ABOUT THE AUTHOR

Sue Edwards was born in Leicestershire and has lived and worked in Yorkshire and Devon. She moved back to her home county in 2018 where she now lives with six dogs, a cat and two ponies. She has two daughters, who live in Leicestershire and Suffolk.

Sue Edwards

RHYMES FROM RURAL ENGLAND

AUSTIN MACAULEY PUBLISHERS™
LONDON • CAMBRIDGE • NEW YORK • SHARJAH

A CIP catalogue record for this title is available from the British Library.

ISBN 9781398439535 (Paperback)
ISBN 9781398439542 (ePub e-book)

www.austinmacauley.com

First Published 2022
Austin Macauley Publishers Ltd
1 Canada Square
Canary Wharf
London
E14 5AA

For Sally and Sarah

POEMS

This poem was written when I had a smallholding and as farms became bigger it became more difficult to make a living from just a few animals. I decided to convert three of our old farm buildings into Holiday Cottages and:

WE DIVERSIFIED

They told us to 'diversify' when farming didn't pay,
To earn another living in a different kind of way;
Now my animals are gone, victims of the Foot and Mouth,
So now we care for tourists seeking fun and sun "down South".

The parlour's now a cottage where the people come to stay,
Now cars park where the tanker came to take the milk away.
Instead of gentle lowing, children shout and play their games,
They stay one week and go. We just get to know their names.

Our cows were our companions and although we had a lot,
We knew all their ways and habits – where to rub their favourite spot.
They would raise their heads to greet us then move slowly to the gate,
They would patiently stand waiting if we happened to be late.

On the other hand, the visitors are here because they've paid
To see the countryside and get a taste of country ways,
But they want their milk delivered and their papers on the mat
And they're horrified to find the internet is not "on tap".

We had to move the chickens 'cos the cockerel crows at dawn
And we had to build a barbecue and a neatly trimmed back lawn.
It takes too long to see the sights because the lanes are narrow
And they got held up this morning by a tractor with a harrow.

They're not keen on the country smells and they hate the muddy lanes
And they'd rather the "facilities" were connected to "the mains".
But it really is so very quaint and the locals – all are charming;
It's really such a pity that they're all involved in farming!

They leave at 10 on Saturday – next guests arrive at two.
I investigate the cooker first and then set about the loo.
We've just four hours to clean it all I peep inside and groan:
Why when they come on holiday, do they leave cleanliness at home?

It varies week to week between a bombsite and a tip,
But every week we get stuck in with scourers, bleach and Jif,
And as I scrub the carpets, make up beds and clean the loo,
How I wish I'd raise my head and hear a friendly moo.

I wish that I was holding not a Hoover but a hose,
And the smell of cows not people was passing up my nose.
I want to hear the tanker pulling up outside the gate;
The driver used to joke about which one of us was late.

But there's no time to stop and think of all that's gone and been;
We've got to keep on scrubbing and get the cottage clean.
The Hoover's put away and everything is back in place;
When the car pulls up outside, I put a smile upon my face.

I welcome to the country city folk in skirts and suits,
And mentally I note that they have not got any boots.
I show them round the cottage, advise on where to eat and drink,
Give directions up to Tesco, which is further than they think!

And then I leave them to it, disappear where I'm not seen;
Say a prayer that they'll be tidy but most of all that they'll be clean.
Then I look across the countryside: that view is free for me;
I do not have to pay to see the country and the sea.

So, although life's changed, I'm lucky visitors just get one week
And then return to smog and noise on their busy city street.
They've remembered the essentials, if it rains they can watch telly,
But as I watch them walk across the fields, I bet they wish they'd brought
some wellies!!

When Covid 19 started to spread across the UK and the country went into lockdown I felt so fortunate to live in such a caring, tranquil village. We all rallied round to help those who couldn't get out and I wrote a series of poems about our Leicestershire village in this trying time.

THE COVID POEM

So – it's here – Coronavirus:
We've been told to stay at home;
Some with houses full of children,
For others all alone.

We've witnessed frantic shoppers
Hoarding tins and toilet roll;
Supermarket shelves are empty,
For some it takes its toll.

But in Hungarton we're lucky,
We have rallied to the task,
With Whatsapp going crazy:
All you have to do is ask.

Our pub is doing takeaways,
Prescriptions fetched and shopping got.
We've mobilised our army,
Between us we can do the lot.

This lovely little village,
Kindly spirits running high;
We look out for each other
And that way we'll get by.

So, when this thing is over,
And – yes – we'll have to wait,
Then my goodness me in Hungarton
We won't half celebrate!!

Another aspect of lockdown was the fact that nobody could get to the hairdressers.

BAD HAIR DAYS

It seems I've missed my chance
To have my hair cut for a while,
But it doesn't really matter:
We're all sporting the same style.

Long and flowing's in,
Short cropped is definitely out.
The Dulux dog is what
My present look is all about.

It's not the length I mind,
The messy look is here to stay.
But it's getting really hard
To try and camouflage the grey.

How I long to get "the treatment",
Sit back while hair is cut and styled,
Have a coffee, read *Hello*,
But that's not happening for a while.

So 'til that "pamper day" arrives
And scissor snip around my head,
I'll have to hide my wayward locks
Beneath a woolly hat instead!!

During lockdown not only did local people help each other but our pub "The Black Boy" provided takeaways for collection or delivery and "Helen's Plants" kept gardeners in the village supplied with shrubs and plants. It felt as if we had everything we needed, so lifting lockdown really didn't impact on our village as it did in other parts of the country.

LIFTING LOCKDOWN

They're lifting the restrictions:
We can socialise with friends.
We must meet up in the garden,
Which is OK 'til it rains.

People rushing to Ikea,
Can't wait to join the mile-long queues.
They are flocking to the seaside
Where no one's opened up the loos.

At Mackie-D's five miles of cars
To get something to eat,
While tailbacks to the tip
Provide another weekend treat.

Garden centres, shops, attractions
Are slowly opening up their doors,
With social distancing a must,
Two-metre markers on the floors.

But in our lovely little village
We don't need to travel far;
Mark and Rachael do our takeaways,
So why go out in the car?

Helen's Plants adorn our gardens
And we have countryside galore.
No need to travel to the seaside
When we've so much to explore.

So yes, the lockdown's lifting,
But let's take it nice and slow,
'Cos in Hungarton we're lucky:
We don't really want to go!!

During lockdown our church clock developed a fault and the villagers were lost without it. It was eventually repaired but not without tensions and argument!!

THE SAGA OF THE CHURCH CLOCK

The church clock had stopped working,
Went into lockdown like us all.
Its chimes were out of sync,
It drove the village up the wall.

So Garry went and stopped it
'Twas the only thing to do;
He'd tried his best to fix it
But he hadn't got a clue.

For 30 years he'd climbed the steps
The clock to tend and care,
But this time it was buggered –
Garry gave up in despair.

Poor Garry he had trod those steps
For all those 30 years.
The fact the clock weren't working,
Well, it drove the man to tears.

Now the villagers weren't happy:
With no clock they all were lost.
Garry had to get it fixed
With no care to the cost.

Meanwhile the Parish Council
Thought the problem they could solve.
So, they tried to fix it too,
And Garry wasn't told.

When the clock repairer came,
The village people were delighted,
So pleased the clock was chiming –
On that they were united.

But behind the scenes a mighty row
Was brewing, over power.
Garry wasn't pleased for 30 years
He'd climbed that bloody tower.

The Parish Council could get lost,
The clock was his to tend.
So now they're in discussions,
But I'm out of time – THE END.

With time on their hands many people turned their hand to growing vegetables. I hope that their efforts went better rewarded than mine!

THE VEGETABLE POEM

Like many during lockdown
The garden's been my daily toil,
Declaring war upon the weeds
And caring for the soil.

In the hope that flowers will bloom,
Creating colour, peace and calm;
A world away from Covid
And keeping safe from harm.

It was going fairly well,
And so I turned my thoughts to veg.
I had a bit of room
Down at the bottom by the hedge.

It can't be very hard,
I was perhaps a little late,
But my thoughts already turned
To a veg stall at the gate!!

With all this excess veg
Which I would grow while on vacation,
I was already getting thoughts and dreams
Way above my station!

With soil-encrusted hands
I planted seeds and plants galore,
But little did I know
Disaster waited at the door.

The long hot spell it drove me on
But veg is different altogether,
'Cos what I hadn't counted on
Was changes in the weather.

The frost it came and went
A lot of seedlings all went black,
But I wasn't going to let
Inclement weather hold me back.

I battled on and things bucked up
Until we had the wind and rain;
The battered plants they just hung on
But they didn't look the same.

I had hoped to be organic –
No such luck with fly and bugs
Of every shape and size;
Don't get me started on the slugs!

But in spite of the disasters
I have harvested some peas;
The broccoli all came at once
And some has gone to seed.

The leeks are looking good,
Tomatoes too are on the way,
But it would seem for now at least
My farm shop trips are here to stay!

Not going into the office proved to be a bonus for some people but not for others. This poem is all about:

WORKING FROM HOME

I've got to wear a dress today,
It's going to be a struggle.
My wardrobe has become
The most horrendous muddle.

I haven't worn a frock in months:
Working from the living room
Means they are just not needed
When we all meet up on Zoom.

These days I dress for comfort:
PJ Bottoms and a sweater.
I slop around in slippers,
No heels – flats are so much better.

And what's more, I take more coffee breaks
Now that I'm staying in;
I'm considering a padlock
To go on the biscuit tin.

The clothes I have don't fit me,
I can squeeze in them if I must.
But I'm quite concerned a cough or sneeze
Could cause a seam to bust.

My hair has not been brushed or combed,
My make up's not been used;
I daren't look in the mirror
I know I wouldn't be amused.

How I long for my clean office
Where all is tidy, nothing lost;
I even miss the constant nagging
Of my overbearing boss.

The input from my colleagues
Makes it less easy to go wrong,
And how the isolation
Makes the day seem very long!

But for now let's find a dress for a Zoom meeting,
Then I'll risk it:
Have an early morning tea break
And another chocolate biscuit.

What a wonderful day it was when a vaccine for Covid 19 was available. The first injections were given on 8th December 2020. A red letter day indeed.

AN END IS IN SIGHT

The scientists have cracked it,
Now we've got a Covid jab.
The first ones in the queue
Will be the likes of Mum and Dad.

It's easy to administer,
A quick jab in the arm,
Then life is back to normal:
You are immunized from harm.

But some folks they are sceptical:
Has the vaccine been too rushed?
They say that it's been tested,
But has it been trialled enough?

And what if there are side effects
Just waiting down the line?
Some need a fuller picture,
These things can take some time.

But for me the answer's simple:
I would like my freedom back.
I have full faith in the scientists
To get us back on track.

I'll be rushing to the surgery
And rolling up my sleeve.
There will be no hesitation
When my name is called – "YES, PLEASE!"

When I first moved into my house in Leicestershire the barn across the yard was boarded up to prevent birds from getting in because they made a mess. One of my first tasks was to take all the boarding off the windows and throw the doors wide open to welcome them back in. I was too late for the first summer but in my second year, the swallows returned. They were so entertaining all summer and I was genuinely sad when they left. Bon voyage little birds: I hope that you will return next year.

MY SWALLOWS ARE GONE

How I will miss their twittering
I'll even miss their mess,
My lovely little swallows
Have up'd and left their nest.

They've started on their journey
So perilous and long;
Now someone else will hear
Their joyous little song.

They worked so hard to build
Their muddy safe and cosy nest,
But now they've gone I'm feeling
Somehow lonely, lost, bereft.

Swooping, diving, flying high,
Hungry mouths to feed;
In and out the barn
At a terrifying speed.

Now travelling to sunnier climes,
But they'll return next year;
And I'll keep looking skywards
Until they reappear.

Some years ago I had a rare breed flock of sheep. It was my first lambing and I was nervous about how I would get on. As it turned out all went well and I eventually ended up with a flock of 300 Poll Dorset ewes and followers. Lambing those few rare breed White Faced Woodlands will always stick in my mind as a turning point in my life.

LAMBING POEM

Lambing time has started ,
The flock are in the shed,
So we can check them in the morning
And before we go to bed.

And just in case there's trouble
We get up in the night
In dressing gown and Wellies
To check that they're alright.

The Ram came down from Bristol,
A fit and firey spark,
So the first lamb should be very soon
Unless he missed his mark.

The sleepless nights, the endless toil,
The feeding up and bedding,
And all with no result:
We start to get a kind of dreading.

Is all this work for nothing?
There must be an easier way
Young Rambo showed such promise:
Could he turn out to be gay?

The villagers are waiting,
They have all heard such a lot
About the ram from Bristol
And this special rare breed flock.

But just when we were feeling
Tired, dejected and forlorn,
We do the usual check to find
One third have lambed that morn!

Well, that's the way to do it –
This 'ere lambing's going a treat.
To lamb a third in just one day,
'Twill be finished by next week.

But this was optimistic,
The rest came by and by.
It felt like we were lambing
'Til the last day of July.

But now, at last, it's over:
Mums and babes out in the field.
The flock size nearly doubled,
Now that's what you call a yield.

"So how many do you have now?"
A friendly voice enquired.
And we answered very proudly:
"At last count, 25!!"

The lane where I live is a dead end and leads down to a footpath and bridleway. In the summer and at weekends it is littered with cars which can sometimes be a problem if a tractor needs to get down to the fields at the bottom. Annoying as this is, I thought about it from the visitors' perspective and this inspired my ramblers poem.

ODE TO RAMBLERS

They come from far and wide
And park out on the lane;
They leave their cars in gateways
And drive you quite insane.

With anoraks and boots and sticks,
A pack upon their back,
They set off on the footpath,
First making reference to the map.

The ramblers have arrived,
Paths, fields and county to traverse;
Will they leave the gates undone,
Or maybe something worse?

But let's just think a moment:
What is here I see for free,
We take it all for granted,
It's just here for folk like me.

I don't have to drive for miles,
To leave the city streets,
To have a few hours in the countryside:
For me this is for keeps.

They may come here from the town
With busy streets, chaos and noise,
Looking forward to their rambles,
Country walks they can enjoy.

So let the ramblers ramble
Enjoy the air and sights I see,
And I will count my blessings,
'Cos that rambler could be me!

There is a farm at the top of the village called Village Farm. The family have farmed the land for several generations in an environmentally friendly way, planting hedgerows, installing underground-source heat pumps to heat the farmhouses and wind turbines for electricity for the farm. Out of the blue they were advised that they would have to have a communications mast. No planning permission is required and the farmer cannot refuse to have it. The only right he has is limited influence over is whereabouts on the farm it is put. As you can imagine, this caused some debate in the village.

MAST DILEMMA

They want to put a mast up
Sky high at Village Farm
To aid communications;
It won't do any harm.

But they don't have to look at it,
It will not spoil their view.
They say that it will benefit
The likes of me and you.

And as for radiation
And any health concern,
Well, they've got to try it out,
That's how the boffins learn.

And yes, the village needs
Fast broadband and a good connection,
And we must think about the future
Before we push for "Mast Rejection".

But can we not communicate
To find some common ground,
Consider pros and cons
Until a compromise is found?

If we must have a mast
Then all opinions should be got:
A bit of consultation,
That's not asking for a lot.

The farmers know the land,
When all is done and said;
Their thoughts should be considered
Before they go ahead.

The politicians they decide
What's right for you and me,
But p'raps this time the village
Should decide their destiny.

We have a monthly village magazine and in one edition we received a contribution from "Mr Grumpy" about what he felt was wrong with modern life, including social media, surveys, celebrity culture and fly tipping. He was, however, a happy person which he said was probably down to the red wine!! I felt very much in tune with his views and the following month I replied in verse.

THE GRUMPY POEM

Having heard from Mr Grumpy
In last month's *Hungarton News*,
It seems I've found at last
A man who shares my views.

Like Mr G I would not want
To stoke up confrontation,
But I feel there's several things
That he has failed to mention.

Packaging is one
Designed to anger and to tease,
Tags to pull or slide,
Lids which should unscrew with ease.

But do they 'eck! You have to reach
For scissors, knives and pliers.
With fingers sore and temper frayed,
You can be struggling for hours.

Dog poo is the other thing
That drives me to despair:
Why can't the owners pick it up?
It's absolutely everywhere!

Now cyclists, their behaviour
Never fails to touch a nerve:
They creep up silently behind you
And then do a frantic swerve.

It seems to me their Lycra
Robs them of the power of speech:
Why can't they just shout, "Bike Behind!"
Before flashing past at speed?

I could go on but time is short,
Like Mr G I've cause to grin,
As life goes on around me,
But I put it down to gin!!

Hungarton is a quiet village with very little traffic. A neighbour has been carrying out some renovations to their cottage and this necessitated digging a hole in the pavement outside. The village was stunned when "Highways" insisted on traffic lights being erected and this state of affairs inspired the following poem.

ODE TO AN 'OLE

"We've got to dig an 'ole," they said,
"It won't take very long
To just bung in a bit of pipe;
10 minutes we'll be gone."

But someone at the Highways
Said, "Not on your Nellie, mate.
This 'ere's a place for traffic lights,
In that there's no mistake.

Rules is rules, lights are required;
It's our job to keep you safe
And help the traffic flow –
Hungarton's a busy place!"

So, the village is in chaos,
A three-way lights control,
And this is all because
We want to dig a bloomin' 'ole.

Then to add insult to injury
The lights stayed on and on;
They didn't come and move them
Although the 'ole was gone.

So, come on, Mr Highways,
Our persecution should be lifted.
In other words, get cracking
And get the blighters shifted!!

I don't have a television which surprises many people. I am also very popular with the TV licensing department who contact me regularly about my lack of a TV licence!!

THE TV POEM

Now I've not got a telly,
Strange I know but true.
The reason is I cannot find
A thing I want to view.

Bake Off, *Strictly* and the Soaps,
I really couldn't bear to look.
I'd rather listen to the wireless,
Knit a jumper, read a book.

I do not need a licence
For a telly I'm not watching,
But try explaining that
To a TV licence boffin.

They just don't seem to get it,
They really cannot see
That I can possibly be happy
If I don't sit and watch TV!!

When I go shopping, I particularly enjoy looking around a market. There is always such a variety of produce and items for sale and the stall holders often enjoy a chat. A visit to my local market on a very cold day was the inspiration behind this poem.

MAKE A MARKET TRADER SMILE

Why do they stand and do it
In the damp and freezing cold,
Wrapped in hats and scarves and mittens?
They look prematurely old.

They start before the dawn breaks
Setting up to sell their wares,
Their displays take time and effort
But no one really cares.

The public rush on by,
They don't take the time to pause.
They want to spend their money
In the large department stores,

Where it's light and warm and airy
And the staff arrive at nine,
They have breaks for tea and coffee
And an hour at dinner time.

Unlike the market trader,
Who is there from dawn 'til night,
Hugging steaming mugs to keep him warm
Until, in fading light,

He packs his wares in boxes,
All the things he hasn't sold,
But he'll be back again tomorrow
To face the rain and cold.

And when you ask them why
It's a way of life, they say:
"Our dads and grandads did it,
They earned a living in this way."

They reminisce about the good days,
How the folks would stand and talk.
They came to town for a day out
For local produce and a walk.

All this before the supermarkets
Came to tempt us with their offers:
"Buy one get one free", it seems,
Has turned us into different shoppers.

So next time you go shopping,
Walk more slowly past the traders;
They have such a lot to offer
And they too have "Super Savers".

Your custom will be valued,
So why not linger for a while?
Take some time to buy it local
And make a market trader smile.

Many years ago, I knew a girl called Jennie who worked at a Residential Home. I think that times have now changed but the residents had a great deal of freedom to come and go and occasionally this caused problems when they "went missing".

ODE TO JENNIE HULMES

This is an ode to Jennie Hulmes,
Who can't keep clients in their rooms.
We seek them here, we seek them there,
They wander off without a care.

They may be old, they may be ill,
But they disappear with oh such skill.
Poor Jennie when she does the rounds,
This now includes the Kenwith Grounds,

She searches every nook and cranny,
Accounting for each wayward granny.
Her hair is grey, her face is fraught,
For all escapees must be caught.

When Miss X up'd and disappeared,
All staff were called 'cos it was feared
That she was gone and no mistake,
But she'd gone paddling by the lake.

When Mr Y went into town
Still in his tartan dressing gown,
He rode his wheelchair down the hill
'Til he got stopped by the "Old Bill".

"What 'ave we 'ere?" the copper frowned,
"From Kenwith Castle, I'll be bound.
Let's call Miss Jennie double quick,
Poor thing, she must be worried sick."

But Mr Y, well he was 'oppin',
He said, "I'm only goin shoppin',
And when I've 'ad me little spree
I'm back to Kenwith for me tea."

The riot van it soon arrived,
And Mr Y was put inside.
They took him back to Kenwith Castle:
"Now you stay here, you wrinkly rascal."

The shift is coming to an end,
Poor Jennie's nearly round the bend.
She checks to see they're all asleep,
False teeth in glasses out to steep.

What a relief it's quiet and still:
Now she can pass them on to Jill.
The time of day that she likes best,
When she goes home and takes a rest,

She thinks about the day she's had:
They really don't mean to be bad,
And after all, it's fair to say
That we will all be old one day.

I think the following poem describes the frustration of a sleepless night many of us have experienced.

YOUR SNORING IS DRIVING ME MAD!!

My husband's sleeping soundly,
While I lay wide awake.
His torturous grunts and snores
Are making bed and covers shake.

My husband's sleeping soundly,
While all I do is toss and turn.
He's quite oblivious that he keeps me
From the sleep that I have earned.

My husband's sleeping soundly,
That's it, I've took all I can take.
I give a shove to turn him over,
I care not if I make him wake.

My husband's sleeping soundly,
So this time I try a poke.
But all he does is cough and splutter
And I almost hope he'll choke.

My husband's sleeping soundly,
And the room is quiet and still.
I lay awake 'cos there's no snoring,
Now I fear he may be ill.

My husband's sleeping soundly,
Now I'm worrying my head:
It's gone so quiet and peaceful,
Will I wake up to find him dead?

My husband's sleeping soundly,
Then through his nostrils snores do seep.
Thank goodness I can close my eyes
And finally go to sleep!

Major construction work has been carried out at a cottage in the village. One day when I walked past I witnessed a rescue which I had to write about in the village magazine.

BUILDERS TO THE RESCUE

The builders have stopped working,
And it's not because of rain.
They're standing scratching heads
And peering down a drain

At a frog and her small froglets
As they frantically swim round.
How on earth did they succeed
In getting so far underground?

Well, there was nothing for it,
As Bert, stripped to the waist,
Lifted up the manhole cover
And fished around in haste.

And so, with Bert laid in the road,
There was a pause in village life.
Everybody came to help or watch
And offer their advice.

His mates came with a bucket
And slow but sure, success!
Mother frog and all her froglets
Rescued from their watery mess.

They took them to the village pond
Where they'll be safe and free from hurt.
They'll live to see another day
And they owe their thanks to Bert.

Well done, guys!

Cars have changed so much since I learnt to drive. I have fond memories of my old MG Midget. We covered many long miles, and I enjoyed every minute. Sadly, those days are gone, and a new era of motoring is around the corner.

RIP MY OLD MG

Leaking oil and engine rattling,
We'd start off in a cloud of smoke.
The fumes were quite enough
To make you cough and choke.

But once out on the open road,
Her engine it would roar,
The smoke and fumes forgotten
As was the broken door.

In her heyday she was fast and sleek,
Racing on mile after mile.
Wind in your hair, this mean machine
Couldn't help but make you smile.

But now we've got to go electric,
No more petrol engines made.
Old cars like mine bound for the scrapheap
As we enter a new phase.

A different type of motoring,
Silent, clean and free from oil.
So good for the environment,
Much better for us all.

No more roaring on the open road,
No more feeling wild and free,
Nor more carefree, hair-blown days,
RIP my old MG.

We are all being advised that we need to be environmentally friendly and recycling has now become a way of life for us all. However, I it can be very difficult to get it right!

RECYCLING WOES

I've sorted the recycling,
The bin's out on the road.
So now I've got to see
If the men will take my load.

Recycling can be stressful,
Not sure if it's just me.
But I feel to do it right
I need to study a degree!

The recycling must be clean,
Tins and bottles should be washed.
To get it in the bin at all
Cardboard boxes must be squashed.

Plastic can be tricky:
Is it coloured, clear or black?
Depending on the Council,
They will sometimes chuck it back.

Cardboard varies too:
Is it a carton or a box?
You need to check,
Although with luck they'll take the bloomin' lot.

If the bin is over-full,
In the wrong place or put out late,
They can refuse to take it
And begging will not change your fate.

The whole thing can depend
On how the bin man's day has gone,
As to whether you have done it right
Or gone completely wrong.

But in the end, we do our bit
To save the planet – heed the warning.
We know that every little helps
To save us all from global warming.

I have always lived in the countryside where hunting is a way of life. It can give rise to heated debate, but I remain neutral on the subject. However, I am always pleased to hear when the fox gets away.

CUNNING MR FOX

Run along now, Mr Fox,
'Cos hounds are on your trail.
You'd better make it quick
If you want to keep your tail.

Horses, hounds and huntsmen:
A country scene, they say.
But I just hope that Mr Fox
Will see another day.

He may have cubs,
A foxy wife.
Run, Mr Fox,
Run for your life.

I saw you just the other day,
My hen house in your view.
I know that you would kill them all
If it were left to you.

But still, I cannot bear the thought
Of a chase through dale and hill;
Over field and stream they will keep on
Before they come in for the kill.

But just by chance you come my way,
My barn door open wide.
As you dash in, I run up quick
And shut you safe inside.

Hounds, huntsmen and their followers
Have had their sport this day;
They admit defeat, their prey has gone,
And so, they ride away.

And as for cunning Mr Fox,
He looks back with a grin.
I need to keep my chickens safe,
That's not the last I'll see of him.

A number of houses in the village, including mine, back onto a small field which is occasionally grazed by sheep. Thereby hangs a tale!

SAM'S SHEEP

Sam's sheep are grazing happily,
He dropped them off and drove away.
He brings them over now and then
For a short holiday.

The villagers all look at them
And Sam comes every day
To check they're being good
And that they do not stray.

Now straying is the problem:
They are contented for a start,
But it doesn't take them long
To find a way they can depart.

It starts with just a head through,
A small gap in the fence,
Then one by one they make a bid
For independence.

They wander up the main street,
Checking gardens as they go;
They stop to graze the verges
And to give your lawn a mow.

The flower beds are tempting,
Just depends on what you've sown,
And if you've got a veg patch
They really make themselves at home.

They are so very friendly
And move on when you shoo them off
To pop next door and have a look
To see what's there to scoff.

Poor Sam he rushes over,
Rounds them up and puts them back,
Apologises to the village
For the gardens they've attacked.

He checks the fence
And carries out repairs to keep them in,
But as he drives away
You can see the sheep all grin.

"We'll stay put for a day or two,
Just keep calm and carry on,
And then we'll all be bored:
He'll come and check and find we're gone!!"

The emphasis is on a greener future and we are all being encouraged to cut our emissions and alter our homes to harness the green revolution.

I AM GOING TO GO GREEN

I'm going to go green,
It's time to bite the bullet.
I've got to sell the trailer,
The electric car won't pull it.

If I want to go long-distance
I will have to use the train,
So, I can think of lots of relatives
I won't be seeing again.

Flying's not an option:
No more holidays in Spain,
I'll have to stay in Blighty
In the cold and wind and rain.

And as for central heating,
That old boiler's got to go,
Replaced with an air source heat pump
And a fancy dynamo.

The windows need replacing,
Double glazing is required,
And it looks like while they're here
I will need to be re-wired.

A wind turbine in the garden,
Solar panels on the lid,
We'll have enough electric
To sell some to the grid.

Insulation will be needed
In the walls and up the attic,
And the pipes could do with lagging,
They can do that while they're at it.

The Aga in the kitchen,
The old wood burner too,
Both have got to go
If I'm going to see this through.

We've got to save the planet
And I have to play my part:
A green revolution's here,
So, it's time I made a start.

I need to go ahead,
Get all the necessary permissions,
To make my home a cleaner place
And reduce all my emissions.

So, when the work is finished,
I'm broke and haven't got a bean,
When I cannot pay the mortgage
It's OK 'cos I've gone green.

I have two children and they were born 18 months apart. I didn't enjoy being pregnant but was overjoyed when my babies arrived. This poem is over 30 years old and was written when I was expecting daughter number two.

THE PREGNANCY POEM

I've found out I'm expecting...
Am I pleased? Well, yes I am.
'Twill be nice to have a brother
Or a sister for our Sam.

The midwife's given me a list
Of things I need to do,
But it isn't quite so simple
With baby number two.

I've been told to take it easy,
If I'm tired to have a nap,
But sleep is hard to come by
With a toddler bouncing on your lap.

Exercise is recommended,
I should take a gentle stroll.
When Sam is in the pushchair
This is easy to control.

But in a minute she is fractious,
Wants to walk all on her own;
By the time she's fallen over twice
We turn round and go home.

Gentle yoga or Pilates
Can be done when she's in bed,
So, I rock her off to sleep
And down the stairs I quietly tread.

All goes well, I am relaxed,
I'm chilling out and feeling fine;
But then I hear a little grunt
Followed by a whine.

It's not long before her screaming
Has got right inside my brain;
It's no good, I'll have to go
And settle her again.

But it's not all bad,
At least I now know what I have to do.
When Sam arrived, it was quite hard,
I hadn't got a clue.

Midnight feeds and nappy changes,
Most nights being kept awake.
Well, this time I'll expect it,
It will be a piece of cake.

And I really cannot wait
For the new babe to arrive.
Two children will be lovely,
I'll walk with one on either side.

But then the unexpected
On the scan 'twas plain to see:
I was not due to have one babe,
I need to get prepared for three!!

When I had my first baby, like many new mothers my life was turned upside down and I really wasn't prepared for it. This poem is about the day that I accidentally left her outside the village shop. It was only for a few minutes. I realized what I had done before I got home and immediately turned round and ran back to fetch her.

A LAPSE IN CONCENTRATION

Oh my God, I've lost the baby!
Can't remember where I've left her.
I recall that she was with me
When I went to post a letter.

We took the dog out for a walk,
She was with me then, I know.
She was strapped inside the pushchair,
There was nowhere she could go.

I really need to find her,
I must track her down with speed.
She will need a change of nappy
And be wanting her next feed.

She isn't in the garden
Where she sits out in the sun.
I've searched the house from top to bottom,
I'm not sure what else can be done.

But then it all comes flooding back:
I went shopping for some jam,
I left her at the village shop,
She's outside in the pram.

I must have picked the dog up,
He was tied up on a hook,
Walked home without the baby.
I never gave a second look.

I ran around the corner
And the pram was in full view.
I peeped underneath the hood
And little Sarah was there too.

Fast asleep and unaware
Of all that had gone on,
Then and there I made a vow
To be a better mom!

For a number of years, I worked as a volunteer for the RSPCA both at the local kennels and as a fund-raiser. It was always sad to see the dogs that were difficult to re-home because they didn't look cuddly or they were afraid and stayed at the back of their kennel.

MR NOBODY

My name is Mr Nobody,
I am lost, I am a stray.
You'll find me in a kennel
At the RSPCA.

My family used to love me
When I was small and fluffy,
But now I've been discarded
I'm no longer cute – I'm scruffy.

I did my best to please them,
We went walking every day.
I ran around the garden,
Entertained them with my play.

But soon they tired of walking,
With the weather turning bad.
They shut me in the garden
Which made me feel quite sad.

They did not want me in the house,
They said I made a mess.
So, they put me in a kennel
Just to add to my distress.

And then one day they took me
In the car and far from home
They threw me out and drove away
And left me all alone.

A kindly passer-by
Heard me cry and howl
And took me to the kennels
Where I am waiting now.

'Cos I'm no longer cute and fluffy,
It will take a while to find
A home where I am loved
And the family are kind.

But I know one day they'll come along,
Someone will choose me in the end,
And they will love me – treat me well
Because I'm man's best friend.

One thing that I have noticed about the Brexit negotiations is that they nearly always seem to involve a meal.

THE BREXIT GRAVY TRAIN

So, we're leaving the EU,
We've hit the Brexit crunch;
Boris Johnson's gone to Brussels
To discuss it over brunch.

It seems the politicians
Cannot agree a deal,
Unless the day involves
Sitting for a hearty meal.

The state of the economy,
Imports, exports – how they're done.
P'raps will break now for elevensies:
Anybody want a bun?

Now you and I consider
A working lunch a treat,
But in Brussels every meeting
Means that there's something to eat.

And the effects of Brexit,
What it means to you and me,
If it's not decided over lunch
They'll thrash it out at tea.

Not sure what's on the menu,
But fishing is up for debate,
And lamb and beef and cheese:
They've got plenty on their plate.

I suppose a little drinkie
Helps to erase their frowns;
After all, they need a wine or two
To help to wash it down.

Back in Blighty we're in tiers,
So, the pubs are shut all day.
We can't go out to swanky restaurants,
We have to have a takeaway!

WE'RE LEAVING

We voted to leave Europe
To become again free nations,
But it seems that we've got nowhere
With EU negotiations.

There are so many stumbling blocks,
So many hopes and fears,
But we're no nearer to a settlement
After four and a half years.

We're told the ports will be bunged up
With stuff that cannot move
Because of problems with the paperwork,
Lorries crammed with rotting food.

They've built extra lorry parks
For all the vehicles down in Kent,
So as they don't block the roads
With goods that can't be sent.

Our food bills will go up and up
Some stuff we will not get
Unless they do a parcel drop
Flying in by jumbo jet.

We are warned of fuel shortages,
No petrol at the station.
No matter – it will help us
Become a greener nation.

But then I think,what is the panic?
We voted to be on our own,
So now we'll have to manage
With all the food that is home-grown.

We don't need imported lamb,
We grow veg and we make cheese.
It's time to rally round our farmers,
They can feed us all with ease.

We will have fish a-plenty,
Milk churns will be overflowing.
We make our own wine too,
In our vineyards grapes are growing.

And yes, it will be different,
We will not have the same choice;
But the EU we are leaving,
We voted with one voice.

So goodbye, Monsieur Barnier,
Boris, come right home,
Leave the EU to negotiate
While we go it alone.

When I first started writing poetry I never dreamed that one day I would be writing one about retirement!!

I'VE RETIRED

So that's it, I've retired:
My working life is done.
I can now look forward
To days of endless fun.

I can do the things I couldn't do,
'Cos I've always been working,
And now if I slow down a bit
I won't be told I'm shirking.

I can lay in bed 'til late,
Not be dictated by the time,
Have lunch out with old friends
And drink that extra glass of wine.

It will be good to see more of the kids
And they'll be pleased, I know,
That I can help out in their gardens
And give their lawns a mow.

I will fill the days with all the jobs
I've always meant to do,
And I'll also now have time
To help a friend or two.

Long days on the golf course,
Catching up on DIY.
The days will pass so quickly,
It will make me wonder why

I took so long to leave the treadmill
Of the long hard, working day.
Oh, I remember now,
'Cos not working doesn't pay!

True, I'll have to watch the pennies,
But I've got some for a rainy day,
And my pension's worth a bit
So, I will be OK.

And will I miss my colleagues,
The worry, work and strife?
Yes, but now it's time to open
A new chapter of my life.

Like many people nowadays I have noticed the large numbers of delivery vans on the road. We often curse them but as our shopping habits have altered, we really only have ourselves to blame.

BE KIND TO OUR WHITE VAN MEN

The white van men are on the road,
They've got no time to lose,
Delivering the packages
And items that we choose.

If you see them on the highway,
Pull over straight away,
'Cos they're delivering our parcels:
They have no time to delay.

And if they can't find an address,
They will frantically be looking,
Rushing fast from house to house.
They can't be late for their next booking.

Hermes, Fast Track, DPD,
They're all on the parcel trail.
What happened to the time
When it was done by Royal Mail?

Parcels large and small
Get to their destinations,
The men leap in and out their vans
Without a moment's hesitation.

And if they see you at the door,
They smile – hold up a hand,
Then throw it in the porch,
Not looking back to where it lands.

I wish that they would take a breath,
Stop for a cup of tea,
But no, they can't, they must rush on
To their next delivery.

When the roads are blocked with vans
And the drivers make us curse,
Don't forget our shopping habits
Are making matters worse.

So next time you're online
And you click because you can,
Please think about the driver
Of the white delivery van.

This poem takes me back to my teenage years when I used to go with my friend Jackie to the local youth club. Sadly, we are no longer in touch, but they were happy days.

DRESSED TO KILL

I used to wear a mini skirt,
It just covered my bottom.
My dad called it a pelmet:
Those days are long forgotten.

Our undies they were skimpy,
We chose our flesh to bare.
We didn't feel the cold,
We didn't have a care.

Any clothing that was sensible
We'd raise our eyes in scorn:
A vest – you must be joking,
We don't need one to be warm.

Eyes thick with mascara,
Red lip gloss on our lips,
Our skirts were tight so as to show
The slim line of our hips.

We were going to the youth club,
There'd by a disco – lots of noise,
But more importantly
We would meet up with some boys.

We'd stand in little huddles,
Weighing up our chances.
The fellas did the same,
Giving us their "come on" glances.

Waiting to be chatted up ,
By the boyfriend of our dreams,
But he wasn't there that evening;
He had other plans, it seems.

But never mind, there'll be next week,
We'll go and to take our chance;
And who knows, Prince Charming may be there
And ask us for a dance.